SUCCESSFUL EVENT PLANNING

Master the art of creating unforgettable experiences

Ray Goodwin

CONTENTS

LIABILITY DISCLAIMER

The information contained within this book is intended for informational purposes only and should not be construed as legal or professional advice. The authors and publishers of this book are not responsible for any losses or damages that may arise from the use of the information contained within.

The reader assumes full responsibility for any decisions made based on the information in this book. The authors and publishers do not endorse any particular method, service or product mentioned in this book and are not responsible for any consequences resulting from their use.

The reader should exercise caution and discretion when making life changing decisions, and should be aware of the risks and potential consequences of their actions. This book is not a substitute for professional or legal advice and should not be relied upon as such.

By reading and using the information in this book, the reader acknowledges and agrees to hold harmless the authors, publishers, and any other parties involved in the creation or distribution of this book from any and all liability, claims, damages, or losses that may arise from their use of the information contained herein.

CHAPTER 1: INTRODUCTION TO EVENT PLANNING

Welcome to the world of event planning! Whether you're an experienced professional or just starting out, this book will guide you through the exciting and challenging process of planning successful events. From weddings to corporate galas, fundraisers to trade shows, we'll cover it all.

My name is Ray Goodwin and I've been in the event planning industry for over 25 years. During that time, I have organized hundreds of events of all shapes and sizes, from intimate gatherings to large-scale productions with thousands of attendees. Through trial and error, I've learned what works and what doesn't, and I'm excited to share my insights with you.

In this book, we will explore the basics of event planning, including budgeting, timelines, vendor management, marketing and promotion strategies. We'll also delve into more advanced topics such as negotiating contracts, managing risk and crisis situations.

So whether you're planning your first event or looking for ways to improve your current approach, let's get started on the path to successful event planning!

Overview

Events are a part of our daily lives irrespective of the scale and nature of the event. Whether it's a birthday party, an office meeting, a political campaign rally or a musical concert, every event is planned, and every successful event is a result of accurate event planning. Event planning, therefore, is the process of bringing together various elements to execute an event successfully.

The process of event planning can involve a lot of hard work, attention to detail, creativity, and a passion for customer service. For many, event planning is an exciting and challenging career that gives them the opportunity to create memorable experiences that bring people together and build relationships.

Types of events

Events can take many forms ranging from social events such as weddings, birthdays and parties to corporate events such as product launch, conferences and meetings. Several kinds of events exist, some of which include personal events, social events, corporate events, and cultural events.

Personal events are events that are about celebrating an individual, such as birthdays and anniversaries. Social events are events that bring people together, such as dinner parties, baby showers, or charity events. Corporate events aim to promote a company's brand and marketing strategies and increase visibility, such as award ceremonies, product launches, or conferences. Cultural events seek to celebrate cultural traditions and encourage the sharing of diverse cultures, such as festivals or religious observances.

Importance of event planning

Every event is unique, and each one requires a different approach to plan successfully. The importance of event planning can't be overstated as it ensures that an event runs smoothly and meets the clients or guests' expectations. The key objective of event planning is to create an experience that resonates with the audience while meeting the client objectives, aligning with the client's budget, and ensuring the event is well-organized.

Successful event planning ensures that an event leaves the guests with a memorable experience and enables organizations to showcase their brand and develop strong relationships with their stakeholders. Well-executed events can also raise funds and generate profit for the event organizers, developing a stable foundation for future events.

Key skills required for event planning

Event planning requires a diverse range of skills to execute an event successfully. These skills include, but are not limited to, budgeting, communication, organization, project management, marketing, and creativity. Attention to detail is an essential skill because proper planning and organization can prevent mistakes, which could have a significant impact on the success of an event.

Responsibilities of an event planner

An event planner can work for a company, an agency, or independently as a freelancer. Irrespective of the work setting, the primary responsibility of an event planner is to oversee that all the elements of an event develop in line with the client expectations and according to budget. An event planner's management includes coordinating vendors, organizing the venue layout, communicating with guests, preparing promotion materials, and ensuring safety and security.

Different roles in event planning

Various roles exist in event planning, working together, such as event coordinators, event production managers, food and beverage managers, audiovisual technicians, event logistics coordinators, and many more. At each event, there is a manager who coordinates the entire planning and execution process.

Overview of the event planning process

Event planning is a process that consists of several stages from conception to execution, including budgeting, scheduling, sourcing, selecting, and managing before and during the event.

First, we begin with event planning. The event planner meets with the client to determine objectives, target audience, event format, budget, and platform required. Next, a team is assembled, and a schedule is created, including the timeline and work schedule for the event.

Budgeting is a crucial aspect that every event planner should consider when planning an event. A clear understanding of the client's budget helps to develop a comprehensive and sustainable event. The event planner must develop a detailed budget which encompasses all aspects of the event from the venue to the décor.

Sourcing and selecting vendors are vital elements in the event planning process and include securing the venue, catering, entertainment, and other peripheral services required for the event.

The event plan stage involves designing the event floor plan, preparing event promotional materials, and having contingency plans in case complications arise.

Common challenges faced by event planners

Event planning is a dynamic and demanding career that often comes with several challenges. Among these are tight deadlines, limited budgets, language barriers, and unexpected occurrences such as bad weather. On top of these, event planners face difficulties such as problematic clients and non-responsive vendors. Challenges arise from the incomplete delivery of services by vendors or the inability to make changes to the schedule at the last minute by clients.

In conclusion, event planning is an intricate process that offers a unique and rewarding career path to individuals interested in events management. With diverse skill sets, a passion to create memorable experiences and a can-do attitude towards challenges, event planners can build successful event management careers. Understanding the importance of event planning, the roles involved in the process, and an overview of event planning challenges are fundamental to the success of an event planning professional.

CHAPTER 2: UNDERSTANDING CLIENT NEEDS

Event planning is all about fulfilling the wants, needs and expectations of your clients and their guests. This chapter examines how to successfully understand and meet your clients' needs.

Identifying Client Objectives

The first step in understanding your clients' needs is identifying their objectives – what they want to accomplish through the event. It's crucial to have a clear understanding of their goals, as this provides direction for all decisions made, and helps to create realistic expectations of the event. Key questions to ask include: What's the purpose of the event? What are the desired outcomes and deliverables? What are the target audience's expectations?

Conducting Client Needs Assessment

Once the client's objectives have been identified, it's important to conduct a thorough needs assessment to clarify their needs. This should involve carrying out a detailed survey to get insights from the client, and conducting focus groups to gather information from their audience.

Budget Constraints

Events can be expensive, and budget constraints often dictate decision making. It's important to get a clear understanding of your client's budget from the onset. Clients will appreciate honesty and transparency from you, as you work with them to create and maintain a budget. As an event planner, be creative and resourceful in finding cost-effective alternatives that will not compromise quality, impact and the event's objectives.

Venue Selection Based on Client Needs

The venue is an essential part of any event, and as an event planner, choosing the right one is critical to accomplishing the client's objectives. The venue should be chosen based on the event's theme and purpose, audience size, location and accessibility. Aspects to consider when selecting a venue include the aesthetics, the availability of equipment and technology, the flexibility to personalize the venue, and the ability to accommodate special or unique requirements.

Communication with Clients

Effective communication is vital when it comes to understanding and meeting the client's needs. Communication should be ongoing and two-way, and should begin by establishing the expectations and objectives from the onset. During the event planning process, regular updates, feedback and revisions should occur so that clients can make informed decisions and adjustments. Communication fosters collaboration, trust, transparency and a sense of assurance between you and your clients to ensure a successful event.

Managing Client Expectations

Understanding client expectations requires an open and honest conversation early in the process, to set the tone and expectations for the event. Clear expectations help manage stress and prioritize requirements for successful event planning. Be cautious about underpromising and overdelivering as it may result in unrealistic expectations from clients, which can lead to dissatisfaction. Set realistic expectations and communicate them clearly, to ensure the overall success of the event while managing client satisfaction.

Building Long-Term Relationships with Clients

Event planning is about building lasting relationships with clients. Creating a positive and memorable experience instills clients with confidence in your abilities and increases the likelihood of continued work, and referral business. Overdelivering and setting realistic expectations show clients that you value their satisfaction and time. Remember to follow up post-event and engage clients on how they perceive the event delivery. Take any feedback given as positive reinforcement or constructive criticism to improve going forward.

Handling Difficult Clients

While the majority of clients will be easy to work with, there will always be some challenging ones. Handling challenging clients requires patience, flexibility and excellent communication skills. Seek to understand their motivations, goals and expectations. Be proactive, keep them informed, stay calm and professional, and work to build a trusting relationship with them through consistency and transparency. Most importantly, tackle any issues early and head-on.

In conclusion, understanding and meeting client needs is critical in the event planning process. By identifying client objectives, conducting a thorough needs assessment, managing budgets, selecting the venue based on the event, developing open communication lines with your clients, managing their expectations, building lasting relationships and handling difficult clients, you can deliver an event that exceeds expectations while building your reputation as a reliable and professional event planner.

CHAPTER 3: CREATING A SUCCESSFUL EVENT PLAN

Creating a successful event plan is often the most critical aspect of event planning. Event planning can be overwhelming, and without adequate planning, the event might not go as planned. Event planning can be compared to building a house, just as a house needs a strong foundation to stand firm, an event needs a well-structured plan to produce a successful outcome. A plan helps you systematically breakdown the event planning process into manageable units, which can help you identify potential problems and create mitigation strategies in advance. In this chapter, we explore essential elements of creating a successful event plan.

Determining event goals

Every event should have a goal, and to create a successful event plan, you must identify and record these goals. Event goals are the primary reason for planning an event and set the tone of the entire planning process. Goals help you focus on what you want to achieve and guide your decision-making process throughout the planning process. Understanding these goals ensures that all event planning and execution is tightly aligned with these goals, thereby assisting in meeting or exceeding them. Once the goals have been identified, they should be documented. This documentation provides a reference point that can help in communicating and articulating the goals to all event stakeholders throughout the planning and execution process.

Establishing timelines and schedules

Timelines and schedules are crucial in the event planning process. To ensure you remain on track and meet your event goals, it is critical to set up a timeline and schedule for the event. The timeline should break down the project into essential tasks that need to be done before, during, and after the event. A well-planned timeline should be informed by the event goals, budgetary constraints, and vendor availability. In addition to creating a timeline, setting deadlines for each task helps the event team remain focused and accountable. Timelines and schedules also ensure everyone involved in the event planning process is aware of their responsibilities and accountabilities.

Creating an event budget

Just like any other project, creating a budget is a crucial component of a successful event plan. A budget is a financial plan that outlines the expected costs, including revenue streams and the items the funds will be used to purchase. An excellent event budget should start with an estimate of what everything will cost, incorporating the expected revenue to determine the net cost of the event. Resources should be allocated based on the goals, priorities, and the amount of available funds. The budget should also take into account potential unforeseen expenses or risks. When creating a budget, it's vital to long-term success to keep track of actual expenses as they accrue and compare them with the budget to ensure you stay within the budget boundaries.

Selecting event vendors

The role of vendors in any event cannot be underestimated.

Vendors can make or break your event. Identifying the right vendors is one of the most crucial decision an event planner can make. Vendors play a crucial role in ensuring the event's success, and the wrong vendor can have catastrophic consequences. However, selecting the right vendor should not be based on familiarity or personal recommendations alone. When selecting vendors, event planners should conduct research, review portfolios, and where possible, conduct site visits to ensure that they align with the event's purpose and theme.

Developing promotional materials

Developing promotional materials is another crucial aspect of an event plan. These materials help create anticipation and excitement towards the event, driving attendance and creating revenue streams. Promotional materials can take many forms, including flyers, posters, social media posts, and advertisements. Developing promotional materials requires creative thinking, a deep understanding of the event's purpose, and a thorough understanding of the target audience. The materials should accurately represent the event and convey the goals and objectives in a clear and concise manner.

Creating a floor plan and event layout

Creating a floor plan forms an essential part of the event planning process. A floor plan and event layout are essential in helping vendors and event planners understand the space in which the event will be held. The floor plan will indicate the dimensions of the space, layout of tables, and the location of vendors. Creating a floor plan is a collaborative process that involves event planners, vendors, and venue staff.

Developing contingency plans

Developing contingency plans should not be an afterthought

in the event planning process. Event planners should develop contingency plans to help prepare for the unexpected. Potential contingencies include power outages, equipment failure, natural disasters, or non-attendance of scheduled performers. The contingency plan should specify what should happen if these occurrences happen, providing a step-by-step process to handle such situations without causing Chaos.

Assessing event success

Assessing event success is essential in determining whether event goals have been achieved. Conducting a post-event evaluation is a critical exercise that shouldn't be ignored. The evaluation can provide insight on essential aspects that contributed to the success or failure of an event. Evaluations should be precise, focusing on the critical aspects of the event. The data collected should be used to make data-driven decisions on future events, applying insights and lessons learned during future events.

In conclusion, the creation of a successful event plan requires a deep understanding and incorporation of all essential aspects that contribute to an event's overall success. Determining event goals, establishing timelines and schedules, creating an event budget, selecting event vendors, developing promotional materials, creating a floor plan and event layout, developing contingency plans, and evaluating event success should be top priorities for event planners seeking to create a successful plan.

CHAPTER 4: EVENT MARKETING AND PROMOTION

As an event planner, your success is largely determined by how well you promote your events to potential attendees. Your marketing plan is critical to ensure attendees, sponsors, and partners know about your event and perceive it positively. This chapter will delve into the different elements of event marketing and promotion that will help make your event a success.

Developing a marketing plan

Before you start promoting your event, it is essential to create a comprehensive marketing plan. This marketing plan should outline your event's major promotional goals, the target audience, and the most effective channels to reach them. Here are some key components you'll want to include in your marketing plan:

- ❖ Event goals: Clarify your event's purpose and objectives, such as raising funds, promoting a product launch, or engaging stakeholders. Knowing your goals will help you determine which marketing channels to use, and the kind of messaging needed to achieve them.

- ❖ Target audience: Define the people most likely to attend your event based on characteristics such as age, gender, interests, and professional background. This will help narrow down the types of channels to use to reach them.

❖ Promotion strategy: Consider how you'll promote your event, including social media, email marketing, and print media.

❖ Budget: Outline how much money you'll spend on promoting your event. Knowing your budget will help you get the maximum return on investment.

❖ Metrics: Establish clear metrics to gauge the success of your marketing plan, such as the number of tickets sold, social media engagement, traffic to your website, and revenue generated. Track these metrics to adjust your marketing plan accordingly.

Creating targeted messaging

Once you have established your marketing plan, it's time to develop the messaging that will resonate with your target audience. Your messaging should focus on what attendees will gain by attending your event and why your event is unique. You want them to feel excited about attending and convey that value proposition in your messaging.

To create effective messaging, you'll need to:

❖ Personalize: Address your audience like you know them personally. By using their names or specifics about their interests, you'll make the message feel more tailored to them, increasing the chances of a response.

❖ Be clear and concise: Your message should be simple, clear, and concise, so that people can quickly understand what your event is all about.

❖ Use visual elements: Use images or videos to make your messaging more visually appealing, making them more likely to engage with them.

❖ Be consistent: Use the same messaging across all your event marketing channels to ensure consistency.

Utilizing social media platforms

Social media is a powerful platform to promote your event. The main social media channels to use are Facebook, Twitter, Instagram, LinkedIn, and YouTube, depending on the target audience.

To effectively use social media for your event, follow these steps:

❖ Plan ahead: Determine what social media channels you want to utilize, and how to create your messaging calendar. Establish key milestones and decide when and what to post in the lead-up to your event.

❖ Use creative elements: Use images, videos, and other visually appealing elements to make your social media posts stand out, and use hashtags and keywords to amplify your message.

❖ Leverage influencers: Work with influencers who have a large social media following and choose influencers whose site or platform is relevant to your event. This will help to reach a larger audience organically.

❖ Use live streaming: Use Facebook Live or Instagram Live to showcase real-time updates from your event, providing an immersive experience for would-be attendees.

❖ Respond to comments: Respond to comments and messages and be available to answer any queries, enhancing engagement with your audience.

Collaborating with sponsors and partners

Collaborating with sponsors is a great way to enhance your event's visibility and reach new audiences. Working with sponsors can give your event the resources it needs to succeed, including financial support, marketing resources, and in-kind contributions.

To collaborate with sponsors and partners, follow these steps:

❖ Identify potential sponsors: Determine businesses and other organizations that align with the theme of your event or have a natural connection to it.

❖ Develop a sponsorship proposal: Once you have identified your potential sponsor, create a sponsorship proposal, which should include details about your event, its goals, and the benefits of sponsoring it. Be sure to provide different levels of sponsorship so that sponsors can choose the level of investment that aligns with their goals.

❖ Finalize a sponsorship agreement: Once you have confirmed a sponsor, finalize the agreement with them by jointly determining their role in the event. This agreement should outline the benefits they will receive, the level of investment, and any other obligations they will have.

❖ Collaborate with partners: Engage with community groups, media houses, bloggers, and other organizations to increase the reach and visibility of your marketing message.

Creating email campaigns

Email campaigns are an effective way to promote your event to people who have already engaged with your organization or attended events in the past. Email campaigns should be personalized and relevant and should communicate the value of attending the event.

To create effective email campaigns, follow these steps:

❖ Segment your audience: Divide your email list into targeted groups based on demographics or interests, and tailor your messaging accordingly.

❖ Write a compelling headline: To increase engagement, make sure to create an attention-grabbing email subject line.

❖ Use visuals: Use images and videos to make your email more engaging and compelling.

❖ Make the email clear and concise: Stick to a clear and concise message and make sure to communicate the key benefits of attending your event.

❖ Include a call-to-action: Make sure to include a clear call-to-action to purchase tickets, download the schedule of events, or share with friends.

Collaborating with media outlets

Collaborating with media outlets is another effective way to promote your event. Local news stations, newspapers, and other media outlets can help to generate interest and buzz for your event and increase your visibility.

To collaborate with media outlets, follow these steps:

❖ Create a press kit: Create a press kit to provide reporters with relevant information about your event, including media releases, images, and videos.

❖ Engage with reporters: Reach out to reporters and engage with them on social media or via email, to discuss the benefits of attending your event and invite them to attend

❖ Submit a press release: Submit press releases to local newspapers and media outlets about the event to increase visibility.

❖ Engage with bloggers: Connect with bloggers and influencers who have a large following or are prominent in your community. Invite these bloggers to attend your event and write about it afterward.

Leveraging influencers

Influencers are people or organizations that have a large following on social media or their website. Working with influencers can help increase your visibility and reach, giving your event a larger audience.

To leverage influencers, follow these steps:

❖ Identify relevant influencers: Research influencers relevant to your event, and determine if their audience aligns with your target audience.

❖ Reach out to them: Once you have identified potential influencers, introduce yourself and explain the benefits of your event and inviting them to attend.

❖ Negotiate the agreement: Once you have agreed to work with the influencer, negotiate the type of promotion that will occur and the benefits the influencer will receive.

❖ Monitor results: Track the success of the influencer campaign, such as the reach of the messaging, sales, and engagement generated.

Tracking results

Once you have promoted your event through different channels, it's important to measure your return on investment and overall success. These results will help you fine-tune your promotional strategy for future event planning.

To track results, follow these steps:

❖   Analyze website traffic: Use Google Analytics or other tools to analyze your website traffic, and identify which channels generated the most traffic and conversions.

❖   Track social media engagement: Track social media engagement through social media analytics to determine which channels are generating the best results.

❖   Monitor email conversion: Use email marketing software to track email open rates and click-through rates to determine the effectiveness of your email campaigns.

❖   Monitor ticket sales: Monitor ticket sales throughout the marketing campaign and analyze the revenue generated, to determine the overall success of your marketing plan.

In conclusion, event marketing and promotion are critical components of a successful event. Creating a comprehensive marketing plan, developing targeted messaging, utilizing social media, collaborating with sponsors and partners, creating email campaigns, collaborating with media outlets, leveraging influencers, and tracking results all play a significant role in promoting your event. By effectively implementing these strategies, you'll ensure that your event reaches a larger audience, generating increased revenue and ultimately greater success.

CHAPTER 5: SITE SELECTION AND LOGISTICS

Site selection is an essential component of event planning. Whether organizing a corporate event or a wedding, selecting the appropriate venue is crucial to the success of an event. However, while many planners focus on finding an ideal venue, they often overlook the logistics of the event. Paying attention to details such as transportation logistics, catering and food service arrangements, and on-site management can significantly enhance the guest experience. In this chapter, we will explore the critical elements of site selection and logistics for event planners.

Venue Selection Criteria

Selecting the right venue is instrumental in creating the desired ambiance and achieving the event's objective. When selecting the venue, consider the type of event, date and time, number of attendees, and budget constraints. Additionally, consider the needs of the attendees to ensure that the venue is accessible and convenient for them. When evaluating potential venues, ask yourself the following questions:

- ❖ Does the venue's style align with the event's theme?

- ❖ Is the venue's location accessible and convenient for most attendees?

* ❖ Does the venue have the necessary amenities and services for the event?

* ❖ Does the venue's capacity accommodate the expected number of attendees?

Conducting Site Visits

Before committing to a venue, conduct a site visit to evaluate the venue's suitability for the event. During the site visit, assess the condition and size of the space, seating arrangements, lighting, sound and video systems, and other production and technical requirements. Meet with the venue coordinator to discuss the details of the event and address any concerns. Additionally, explore the surrounding area to ensure that there are restaurants, hotels, and entertainment options for the guests.

Reviewing Venue Contracts

When signing a venue contract, ensure that the contract clearly outlines the terms and conditions of the rental. The contract should include the date and time of the event, the rental fee, the refund policy, and any additional costs such as security or cleaning fees. Ensure that the contract addresses any specific requirements such as catering arrangements, decorations, and alcohol service.

Production and Technical Requirements

Events often require specific production and technical requirements such as audio and video systems, lighting, and stage construction. Ensure that the venue has these capabilities and work with the venue coordinator to coordinate the arrangements. Additionally, consider hiring a professional production company to provide the necessary equipment and expertise.

Transportation Logistics for Guests and Staff

Transportation is a critical component of event planning, especially for events held in urban settings. Consider the transportation needs of the attendees and staff, including parking options, shuttle services, and public transportation. Additionally, consider the transportation logistics for any VIP attendees or performers.

Catering and Food Service Arrangements

Food and beverage service is a significant aspect of event planning, and it is essential to consider the type of event, the time of day, and the number of attendees when selecting the menu. Work with the venue coordinator or a professional catering company to design a menu that meets the needs and preferences of the guests. Additionally, ensure that the catering service aligns with the event's theme and style.

Event Registration and Check-In

Event registration and check-in are crucial components of event planning that contribute to the guest experience. Ensure that the registration and check-in process is fast, efficient, and user-friendly. Provide clear instructions and directions, and ensure that the staff is trained to handle any issues or concerns.

On-Site Management and Coordination

On-site management and coordination are essential components of event planning that ensure the event runs smoothly and meets the guests' needs. Work with the venue coordinator or hire an event coordinator to manage the different aspects of the event such as production, technical support, catering, and guest services. Additionally, ensure that the staff is trained to handle any issues or concerns that arise during the event.

Conclusion

In conclusion, event planners must pay close attention to the site selection and logistics of an event to ensure the overall success of the event. By selecting the appropriate venue and coordinating the logistics of the event, planners can create a seamless and enjoyable experience for the guests. Remember to conduct site visits, review contracts, and coordinate catering, transportation, and registration services. With these elements in place, your event is sure to leave a lasting impression on your guests.

CHAPTER 6: CREATING ENGAGING EVENT CONTENT

Creating engaging content is an important aspect of event planning. It can help you to capture and maintain the attention of your attendees and ensure that your event is memorable. In this chapter, we will discuss how to create engaging event content that resonates with your audience.

Determining the Event Theme

The event theme is the primary idea or message that you want to communicate to your attendees. It sets the tone and direction for your event. When creating an event theme, consider what your attendees expect from the event and what message you want to convey. A strong event theme will ensure that your attendees have a clear understanding of the event's purpose and what they can expect to gain from attending.

Developing Event Presentations

Presentations are a great way to communicate ideas and information to your attendees. Strong presentations are engaging, informative, and visually appealing. When developing presentations, consider the following:

❖   The purpose of the presentation – what message or information do you want to convey?

❖   The medium – will you be using slides, videos, or other interactive elements?

❖   The audience – who will be attending, and what is their level of expertise on the topic?

❖   The timing – how long should the presentation be, and at what point in the event should it take place?

Selecting Keynote Speakers

Keynote speakers can add tremendous value to an event. They can provide unique insights and experiences, inspire attendees, and help to make the event memorable. When selecting a keynote speaker, consider the following:

❖   The topic – does the speaker have expertise on a relevant and valuable topic?

❖   The delivery – is the speaker engaging and dynamic, and do they have experience speaking in front of large audiences?

❖   The audience – does the speaker resonate with the event's audience?

❖   The timing – when is the best time during the event to schedule the keynote speech?

Creating Interactive Experiences

Interactive experiences can be highly engaging and memorable for attendees. They can help to foster connections between attendees, increase participation, and provide valuable learning opportunities. When designing interactive experiences, consider the following:

- ❖ The purpose – what message or information do you want to communicate, and how will the interactive experience help to achieve that?

- ❖ The format – will the experience be group-based, individual, or a combination of both?

- ❖ The timing – when in the event should the interactive experience take place, and how long should it last?

- ❖ The facilitation – who will facilitate the interactive experience, and how will attendees be guided through the experience?

Identifying Entertainment Options

Entertainment options can add value and excitement to an event. They can help to set the tone, provide a break from more serious content, and keep attendees engaged. When identifying entertainment options, consider the following:

- ❖ The audience – what type of entertainment would resonate with the event's audience?

- ❖ The timing – when in the event should entertainment take place, and for how long?

- ❖ The message – does the entertainment align with the event's purpose and message?

- ❖ The budget – what is the cost of the entertainment, and does it fit within the event's budget constraints?

Incorporating Visual and Audio Elements

Visual and audio elements can enhance the overall experience of an event. They can help to create a more immersive experience, convey information in a dynamic way, and engage multiple senses. When incorporating visual and audio elements, consider the following:

- ❖ The purpose – what message or information do you want to convey through the visual and audio elements?

- ❖ The timing – when during the event should the elements be used, and for how long?

- ❖ The technology – what technology is needed to create the desired visual and audio effects?

- ❖ The logistical considerations – what needs to be done to ensure that the visual and audio elements are seamlessly integrated into the event?

Creating Engaging Activities

Engaging activities can help to break up the event and keep attendees energized and engaged. When creating engaging activities, consider the following:

- ❖ The purpose – what message or information do you want to convey through the activities?

- ❖ The timing – when during the event should the activities take place, and for how long?

- ❖ The team-building aspect – can the activities help to build relationships and connections between attendees?

- ❖ The diversity – are there a variety of activities that will appeal to different preferences and demographics?

Developing Immersive Experiences

Immersive experiences are highly engaging and can create a lasting impression on attendees. They can provide a unique and memorable way to convey a message or experience. When developing immersive experiences, consider the following:

❖ The theme – does the immersive experience align with the event's theme?

❖ The purpose – what message or information do you want to convey through the immersive experience?

❖ The logistical considerations – what needs to be done to ensure that the experience is well-executed and seamless for attendees?

❖ The cost – is the immersive experience within the event's budget constraints?

In conclusion, creating engaging event content is an essential part of event planning. It helps to create a memorable event experience and ensures that attendees are engaged and focused. By considering the purpose, audience, timing, and logistics, event planners can create engaging event content that resonates with their attendees and achieves the desired outcomes.

CHAPTER 7: MANAGING FINANCES

One of the biggest challenges faced by event planners is managing finances. Event budgets can easily get out of hand, especially if expenses are not monitored closely. Effective financial management is essential for a successful event. Event planners need to be knowledgeable about budgeting, accounting, and managing vendor payments. In this chapter, we will discuss the key steps in managing finances for an event.

Preparing a Comprehensive Budget

The first step in managing finances for an event is to prepare a comprehensive budget. The budget should include all potential expenses and income sources. This includes venue rental, catering, decorations, entertainment, transportation, and marketing expenses. Other potential costs may include permits, licenses, insurance, and staffing costs. It's important to identify all potential expenses that may arise during the event planning process and account for them in the budget.

When creating a budget, it's important to establish a clear idea of the client's expectations and goals for the event. This will help determine the budget requirements for each aspect of the event. It's important to set a realistic budget and ensure that there are enough funds to cover all expenses. It's also important to plan for unexpected costs that may arise during the event planning process.

Allocating Funds Effectively

Once the budget has been established, it's important to allocate funds effectively. This means ensuring that the budget is adequate to cover all planned expenses and contingencies. It's important to allocate funds appropriately, and prioritize expenses based on their importance to the success of the event.

Budget allocation should be based on the client's priorities. For example, if the client's goal is to host a high-end event with top entertainment, then a larger budget allocation should be made for these expenses. Similarly, if the client's budget is limited, then expenses should be prioritized based on their importance to the event's success.

Maintaining Financial Records

Effective financial management requires accurate financial record-keeping. It's important to keep track of all income and expenses, and to reconcile these records regularly. Having detailed financial records can help identify areas where costs can be reduced, or expenses can be optimized. Detailed financial records also provide valuable information for future events.

Managing Vendor Payments

Managing vendor payments is an important aspect of financial management. Ensure that payments are made on time to avoid any potential issues. Payments should be made according to the vendor contract terms and conditions. It's important to keep accurate records of payments made and to reconcile these records regularly. Any discrepancies or issues should be addressed immediately to avoid potential conflicts.

Reconciling Accounts

Reconciling accounts is a key step in effective financial management. This involves comparing financial records with bank statements and invoices to ensure accuracy. Any discrepancies should be investigated immediately and addressed.

Tracking Expenditures and Income

Tracking expenses and income is essential for effective financial management. This includes keeping track of all income sources such as ticket sales, sponsorships, and donations. For expenses, it's important to keep a detailed record of every cost incurred, including receipts, invoices, and contracts. This helps identify areas where costs can be optimized and provides valuable information for future events.

Managing Unexpected Costs

Unexpected costs can arise during the event planning process. It's important to plan for these contingencies in the budget. However, if unexpected costs do arise, it's important to manage them effectively. This may require identifying areas where costs can be reduced, identifying alternative suppliers or solutions, or adjusting the budget allocation accordingly.

Securing Sponsorships

Securing sponsorships is a key part of event financing. Sponsors can provide valuable financial support for the event and may also offer access to valuable resources such as speakers, venues, or equipment. When seeking sponsorships, it's important to identify potential sponsors that align with the event's goals and values. A well-planned sponsorship package can be an effective way to secure financial support from sponsors.

Conclusion

Effective financial management is essential for a successful event. This requires careful budgeting, effective allocation of funds, detailed financial record-keeping, and effective management of vendor payments and unexpected costs. Additionally, securing sponsorships can provide valuable financial support for the event. By following these guidelines, event planners can manage finances effectively and ensure a successful event.

CHAPTER 8: EVENT SPONSORSHIP AND FUNDRAISING

Event sponsorship and fundraising are essential for the success of any event, whether it is a small gathering or a large-scale event. Sponsorship not only provides additional funding for your event but also creates opportunities to build relationships with other organizations and promote your brand. In this chapter, we will discuss how to identify potential sponsors, create sponsorship packages, and develop fundraising strategies for your event.

Identifying Potential Sponsors:

The first step in securing event sponsorship is to identify potential sponsors. Start by researching companies and organizations that align with the goals and themes of your event. Consider the type of event you are planning and its target audience. Which businesses would be interested in reaching that audience? Look for companies that have a history of sponsoring similar events or have expressed an interest in sponsoring events like yours.

You can also consider partnering with complementary businesses or vendors that offer services or products related to your event. For example, if you are planning a health and wellness fair, you might consider partnering with a gym, a sports equipment store, or a health food shop. This type of partnership not only provides financial support but also adds value to the event for attendees.

Creating Sponsorship Packages:

Once you have identified potential sponsors, it is essential to create sponsorship packages that provide value for them. Sponsorship packages should be tailored to the specific needs and interests of each sponsor and clearly outline the benefits of sponsorship. Consider offering various sponsorship levels to accommodate different budgets and goals.

Some common benefits of event sponsorship include prominent branding and signage at the event, inclusion in promotional materials such as flyers and social media posts, and the opportunity to speak or present at the event. You may also consider providing the sponsor with a booth or table to promote their products or services and offering tickets or access to the event for their employees or clients.

When creating the sponsorship package, be sure to clearly outline what each sponsor will receive and what their contribution will be. It is important to be transparent about where their money is going and how it will be used.

Developing Fundraising Strategies:

In addition to event sponsorship, fundraising is another essential aspect of event planning. Depending on the type of event, fundraising can involve anything from ticket sales to silent auctions and raffles.

When planning your fundraising strategy, consider the interests and preferences of your audience. For example, if you are organizing a charity event, you might consider setting up a giving wall where attendees can donate money in exchange for writing their name or a message on a board. You can also consider partnering with local businesses to donate items or services for a raffle or auction.

Social media can also be an effective tool for fundraising. Consider creating a social media campaign that encourages attendees to donate to your cause or organization. You can also consider utilizing crowdfunding platforms such as Kickstarter or GoFundMe to raise funds for your event.

Negotiating Sponsor Contracts:

Once you have identified potential sponsors and created sponsorship packages, it is time to negotiate the terms of the sponsorship agreement. When negotiating sponsor contracts, it is important to be clear about what each party expects from the other. Consider hiring a lawyer to help negotiate and review the contract to ensure that it is fair and legally-binding.

Be sure to outline the start and end date of the contract, the amount and type of sponsorship, and the benefits that the sponsor will receive. It is also important to outline any exclusivity agreements or restrictions on competitors in the same industry.

Leveraging Sponsorship Benefits:

Once you have secured event sponsorship, it is important to leverage those benefits to encourage attendees to attend and promote the event. Consider including sponsor branding in your promotional and marketing materials, including email campaigns and social media posts.

You can also use sponsor benefits to incentivize attendees. For example, if a sponsor is offering a discount or promotional offer, promote it to attendees to encourage them to participate in the event. Additionally, consider creating opportunities for sponsors to engage with attendees, such as hosting a booth or table where they can showcase their products or services. This not only provides value for the sponsor but also adds value for event attendees.

Fundraising strategies can also be leveraged by promoting the event as a fundraising opportunity. Consider creating a leaderboard or tracker for fundraising efforts and promoting the leaderboard on social media to encourage attendees to donate.

Conclusion:

Event sponsorship and fundraising are critical components of successful event planning. Identifying potential sponsors, creating tailored sponsorship packages, and developing effective fundraising strategies can help you secure financial support and build relationships with other organizations. By negotiating sponsor contracts and leveraging sponsor benefits, you can promote your brand and encourage attendees to participate in the event.

CHAPTER 9: EVENT OPERATIONS AND LOGISTICS

Event operations and logistics play a key role in making sure that an event runs smoothly. Even the smallest task or detail can impact the overall success of the event. This chapter will focus on the various aspects involved in event operations and logistics, including coordinating event staff, managing vendor relationships, ensuring safety and security, managing transportation logistics, coordinating on-site catering and food service, handling registration and check-in processes, overseeing guest services, and managing event emergencies.

Coordination of Event Staff:

Event staff forms the backbone of any successful event. They carry out various tasks, including setting up and tearing down the event, managing logistics, providing guest services, and ensuring the smooth running of the event. It is important to ensure that the event staff is properly trained and managed to ensure that they carry out their roles efficiently.

Before the event, the event planner should develop and communicate detailed roles and responsibilities for the staff. If the planner has a team of staff already, he or she needs to delegate duties based on individual skills and interests. A good event planner should avoid leaving things to chance as this increases the likelihood of confusion and disorganization on the day of the event.

On the day of the event, the event planner should ensure that all staff members have a clear understanding of what is expected of them, their roles, and the chain of command in case of any issues. This will ensure that everyone is on the same page and working towards a common goal.

Managing Vendor Relationships:

Vendor relationships are important to ensure that an event runs smoothly. Examples of vendors include catering companies, equipment rental companies, and transportation providers. Effective vendor management involves ensuring that vendors deliver quality services, on time, and within budget. It also involves developing good relationships and negotiating fair terms.

The event planner should first identify vendors who work within the event's budget and are capable of delivering the required service. Choosing vendors who understand the event's goals and have experience working in similar events will also help to ensure a smoother event operation.

Once vendors are identified, the event planner should establish written agreements laying out their scope of work, payment terms, and delivery times. It is also important to maintain good communication with vendors throughout the planning process to avoid misunderstandings and identify any potential issues.

Ensuring Safety and Security:

Safety and security are integral components of event planning and logistics. By taking preemptive measures, the event planner can ensure the safety of the attendees and staff, as well as prevent any potential security threats.

In the weeks leading up to the event, the event planner should carry out a thorough risk assessment and develop a risk management plan. This should include identifying potential risks and hazards that may occur before, during, or after the event, and developing a strategy to minimize or eliminate them.

The event planner should also identify and work with local authorities and emergency response teams to come up with a contingency plan in case of any emergency. In addition, the event planner should ensure that all staff members are trained on how to handle emergencies.

Managing Transportation Logistics:

Proper transportation planning is important to ensure that attendees arrive at the event on time. The event planner should first identify the mode of transportation that will be used, whether it is personal cars, public transportation, or shuttles. Once the mode of transportation is identified, the event planner should establish transportation schedules and determine the number of vehicles or buses required.

In addition, the event planner should also identify the location of parking lots or areas designated for transportation. This will help minimize traffic flow around the venue.

Coordinating On-Site Catering and Food Service:

Catering is an important aspect of any event, and it is important to ensure that attendees have access to quality food and beverages. The event planner should work with a reputable catering company that has experience in providing services for events.

The event planner should communicate the catering requirements to the catering company, including the estimated number of attendees, dietary restrictions, and menu preferences. Once the contract is signed, the catering company should be provided with a detailed event schedule, so they can plan accordingly.

Handling Registration and Check-in Processes:

Registration and check-in are critical components of event logistics. Attendees need to check-in for badges and credentials, and the process must be efficient and fast. This ensures that attendees have ample time to participate in all the activities planned for the event.

The event planner should first develop an online registration system that is easy to use and is clearly communicated with attendees. Once on-site, attendees should have a designated area for registration and check-in, with staff members available to handle any inquiries and issues.

Overseeing Guest Services:

Guest services play a critical role in ensuring that attendees feel comfortable and welcome at the event. Guest services may include directing attendees to their designated parking spots, providing a guide or map of the event, or providing additional information about the event.

The event planner should ensure that all necessary staff members are designated to handle guest services. The staff members should be trained on how to address any inquiries and issues that may arise during the event.

Managing Event Emergencies:

Despite all the precautions and preemptive measures taken, emergencies may still occur during the event. The event planner should develop a contingency plan to deal with any event emergencies.

The contingency plan should include clear responsibilities for the event staff, a detailed communication plan, and a chain of command in case of an emergency. The plan should also include emergency contact numbers for local authorities, emergency response teams, and medical professionals.

Conclusion:

Event operations and logistics play a critical role in ensuring that an event runs smoothly. Proper coordination of event staff, effective vendor management, ensuring safety and security, managing transportation logistics, coordinating on-site catering and food service, handling registration and check-in processes, overseeing guest services, and managing event emergencies are all crucial aspects that should be taken into consideration when planning an event. By taking a comprehensive and proactive approach to event operations and logistics, an event planner can ensure that the event meets its objectives and runs efficiently.

CHAPTER 10: PLANNING LARGE-SCALE EVENTS

Large-scale events require a different level of planning and execution as compared to smaller events. These events may include music festivals, sport tournaments, multi-day conferences, or any other event that hosts a large number of attendees. Large-scale events need comprehensive planning in all aspects of the event, ranging from venue selection to on-site logistics management. Event planners must bring their A-game and work diligently to ensure everything runs smoothly. This chapter discusses the unique challenges of large-scale events and how event planners can effectively plan and execute such events.

Defining large-scale events

Large-scale events are defined as those that host more than 1,000 attendees. These events require significant logistical coordination, management, and execution. Such events usually have a considerable economic impact on the surrounding communities, and as a result, they attract a range of stakeholders that should be taken into account. Therefore, successful planning is crucial to ensuring the event runs smoothly, all stakeholders are satisfied, and any negative consequences are mitigated.

Unique challenges of planning large-scale events

Large-scale events pose significant challenges to event planners due to their size, complexity, and the number of stakeholders involved. These challenges include:

❖ Organizational complexity: Hosting large-scale events involves coordinating multiple aspects, such as transportation, catering, security, ticketing, and marketing, among others. Event planners need to put in place systems and processes that can manage all these complexities.

❖ Budget constraints: Large-scale events usually come with significant financial outlays that sometimes require the organizers to seek sponsorship deals to make the event financially viable.

❖ Risk management: Large-scale events present higher-than-usual risks, ranging from safety concerns for the attendees, damage to the environment, and other potential liabilities that could lead to significant losses. Event planners must develop and implement adequate risk management and contingency plans.

❖ Stakeholder management: Because of the larger scale of the event, a large number of stakeholders are involved. These stakeholders include sponsors, vendors, suppliers, security, attendees, and local authorities, among others. Managing all these stakeholders, and responding to their needs and concerns, presents a significant challenge to the event planner.

Creating a comprehensive plan

The planning process for large-scale events should be comprehensive and collaborative. The following steps can be taken to develop a comprehensive plan for large-scale events:

❖ Establish the event goals: Define the overall purpose and objectives of the event, taking into account the needs of all the stakeholders involved.

❖   Develop an event vision: Develop a vision statement that defines the desired outcomes of the event.

❖   Identify the target audience: Define the type of audience you want to attract to the event, and adjust the event offerings based on their preferences.

❖   Determine the event theme: Develop an event theme that resonates with the audience and aligns with the event's goals.

❖   Plan the event timeline: Develop a timeline that outlines the major milestones, deadlines, and timelines for various components of the event.

❖   Select the event venue: Based on your event goals and objectives, select a venue that meets your requirements in terms of space, location, and capacity.

❖   Manage multiple vendors: Select reliable vendors that can manage their aspects of the event, such as catering, lighting, decoration, and security, among others.

❖   Develop a contingency plan: Develop a contingency plan that outlines what to do in case an unlikely event occurs during the event, such as a medical emergency, natural disaster, or any other issue that could harm the attendees or cause a disruption to the event.

❖   Ensure compliance with regulations: Ensure compliance with all local regulations and laws concerning events, including permits, licenses, and insurance.

❖   Budget for the event: Develop a comprehensive budget for the event, which includes all aspects of the event, including marketing, vendor costs, venue rental fees, security expenses, and production costs, among others.

Managing multiple vendors

Large-scale events involve multiple vendors, each handling a specific portion of the event. These multiple vendors pose a management challenge for event planners. However, managing multiple vendors can be easier with the following tips:

❖ Assign roles and responsibilities: Communicate roles to each vendor and give them clearly defined responsibilities. This approach helps to avoid confusion and redundancies.

❖ Develop vendor guidelines: Develop vendor guidelines, including timelines for deliverables and clear processes for relationship management.

❖ Facilitate communication: Develop efficient communication channels to enable easy communication between the vendors.

❖ Conduct regular check-ins: Conduct regular check-ins with the vendors to ensure that deadlines are being met, and issues are being addressed.

Conducting risk assessments

Risk assessments enable event planners to identify hazards, assess the likelihood of occurrence, and evaluate the potential impacts. Risk assessments are essential for large-scale events since a significant amount of resources and money are at stake. Event planners should engage in the following steps to conduct thorough risk assessments:

❖ Identify risks: Identify potential risks in all aspects of the event, including vendor selection, site selection and logistics, safety and security, communication, and marketing.

❖ Assess risks: Evaluate the likelihood of occurrence and the potential impact of each identified risk.

❖ Develop a mitigation plan: Develop a mitigation plan that outlines how to prevent the risks from occurring or reduce and manage their impacts.

❖ Train staff: Ensure that all staff involved in event planning are aware of the risks and the mitigation plans, including contingency plans.

❖ Continuously monitor risks: Monitor the risks up to and during the event.

Budgeting for large-scale events

Budgeting for large-scale events requires a comprehensive approach since considerable resources are involved, and it is essential to avoid shortages or going over-budget. Below are tips that can help in budgeting for large-scale events:

❖ Develop a comprehensive budget: Create a comprehensive budget that includes all aspects of the event, from marketing to vendor costs.

❖ Allocate budget efficiently: Allocate the budget effectively based on the priorities of the event, making sure that all aspects of the events are covered.

❖ Track expenses: Track all expenses and ensure that they stick to the budget.

❖ Prepare for contingency expenses: Prepare for the unexpected expenses that were not accounted for in the initial budget.

Logistics for large-scale events

Managing logistics for large-scale events involve coordinating multiple activities and vendors. Proper logistics management can be achieved by implementing the following tips:

- ❖ Plan well in advance: Start planning logistics early to ensure all details can be adequately managed.

- ❖ Assign a logistics manager: Appoint someone to oversee logistics management, ensuring that everything is running smoothly.

- ❖ Coordinate with vendors: Coordinate with all vendors to identify their needs and ensure that all aspects of their requirements are understood and delivered.

- ❖ Develop contingency plans: Develop contingency plans to handle any problems that may arise during the event.

- ❖ Provide effective communication channels: Develop communication channels that ensure all stakeholders can be easily communicated to before and during the event.

Conclusion

Successfully planning and executing a large-scale event requires different skills and approaches than smaller events. Event planners must remain meticulous and pay attention to every detail at every stage of the event. By following the tips given above, event planners can effectively plan and execute large-scale events that meet stakeholders' needs, stay on budget, and exceed audience expectations.

CHAPTER 11: TECHNOLOGY IN EVENT PLANNING

In today's digital age, event planning has been revolutionized by the use of technology. The availability of numerous tools and software has transformed the way events are conceived, designed, and executed. From mobile apps to virtual and augmented reality, technology has enabled event planners to create engaging experiences that captivate attendees and enhance event outcomes. In this chapter, we will explore how event planners can utilize technology to enhance their events and ensure success.

Identifying Relevant Event Technology

With hundreds of technology tools available for event planning, selecting the right ones can be overwhelming. As an event planner, it is important to identify the technologies that will enhance your event goals and objectives. Some common types of event technology include:

❖ Mobile Apps - Mobile apps have made event planning and management easier and more efficient. They can be used to facilitate event registration, provide event information, allow for easy navigation through the event spaces, and provide instant feedback and ratings. Mobile apps can also be used to push event updates, integrate social media feeds, and provide real-time analytics.

❖ Event Management Software - This type of software is designed to streamline event management processes, including attendee registration, budget planning, vendor coordination, program scheduling, and data analysis. Event management software is essential for large-scale events as it allows for improved communication, data tracking, and real-time updates.

❖ Virtual and Augmented Reality - Virtual and augmented reality technology can enhance the overall attendee experience by creating immersive experiences that are not possible with traditional event setups. This technology can be used to create 3D visualizations of event spaces, enabling attendees to virtually tour an event location before attending. Virtual reality technology can also be used to create unique educational experiences, such as virtual tours of manufacturing facilities, or medical procedures.

Creating Engaging Virtual Experiences

The COVID-19 pandemic has accelerated the trend towards virtual events, and event planners must adapt to this new reality. The success of virtual events depends on the ability of event planners to create immersive, engaging experiences that meet the expectations of attendees. One key challenge in virtual event planning is creating an experience that can replicate the feel of a live event, including networking opportunities and the sense of community.

One strategy to improve attendee engagement in virtual events is to create interactive virtual experiences. This includes creating virtual booths, virtual reality experiences, and live streaming sessions with interactive chat capabilities. Another approach is to utilize gamification techniques to engage participants. Gamification involves creating games or activities that encourage attendee participation, such as competitions, polls, and quizzes.

Integrating Event Technology with Event Planning

The integration of event technology with event planning requires careful planning and coordination. When selecting event technology, it is important to ensure that it aligns with the event goals and objectives. It is also important to ensure that the technology is accessible to all attendees, including those with disabilities.

As event technology is constantly evolving, event planners must keep up to date with the latest trends and developments. This can be done through attending industry events, following relevant blogs and forums, and participating in industry associations.

Tracking Event Data and Analytics

Event data and analytics are essential in measuring the success of an event. Data collected from attendees can be used to assess their overall satisfaction with the event and identify areas for improvement. Such data can also be used to optimize the event in real-time, addressing any issues that may arise during the event.

One strategy to collect data and analytics is to utilize event management software that allows for real-time data collection. This type of software can be used to track attendee behavior, measure event engagement, and assess the effectiveness of individual sessions or presentations. Another approach is to utilize social media analytics to track virtual interactions and engagement.

Enhancing Attendee Engagement with Technology

Technology can be used to enhance attendee engagement in numerous ways, such as creating interactive presentations, gamification, and customized online experiences. One effective way to engage attendees is through creating dynamic visuals and presentations. This can include creating interactive booths, live streaming presentations, and using augmented or virtual reality tools.

Another strategy is to use social media platforms to create a sense of community among attendees. This can be achieved through setting up private groups for attendees to share information and network. Social media can also be used to facilitate attendee feedback and engagement.

Managing Tech-related Risks

Technology can come with certain risks that event planners must consider, such as data breaches, system failure, and cyber-attacks. Event planners must be proactive in managing these risks, ensuring that proper protocols and security measures are in place to protect attendees and event data.

One strategy is to ensure that all data collected is encrypted and secure. This includes data collected through event registration forms, social media platforms, and mobile apps. It is also important to implement robust cybersecurity measures, such as firewalls, antivirus software, and intrusion detection systems.

Conclusion

Technology has become an essential part of event planning, enhancing attendee experiences and improving event outcomes. From mobile apps to augmented reality, event planners must stay up to date with the latest technology trends and developments. The integration of technology with event planning requires careful planning and coordination, ensuring that it aligns with the event goals and objectives. Finally, event planners must be proactive in managing tech-related risks, ensuring that attendee data and privacy are protected.

CHAPTER 12: SUSTAINABILITY IN EVENT PLANNING

Sustainability in event planning has become an increasingly important area of focus over the past decade. Event planners must prioritize sustainability in order to reduce their carbon footprint and promote environmentally-friendly practices. In this chapter, we will explore what sustainability means in the context of event planning, identify sustainable event practices, and discuss the different ways in which event planners can reduce waste and promote sustainable practices.

Defining Sustainability in the Context of Events

Sustainable event planning refers to the integration of environmental, social, and economic considerations into all aspects of event planning, management, and production. In other words, sustainable event planning is about minimizing the environmental impact of events, while also promoting social and economic sustainability. Event planners must take into account the different factors that contribute to the environmental impact of events, including energy consumption, waste production, and carbon emissions.

Identifying Sustainable Event Practices

There are a variety of sustainable event practices that event planners can implement in order to reduce their events' environmental footprint. Some of these practices include:

❖   Reducing paper waste: One of the easiest ways to reduce the environmental impact of events is to minimize the amount of paper used. Event planners can switch to digital invitations, tickets, and programs, instead of printing physical copies.

❖   Reducing water waste: Event planners can reduce water waste by implementing water-saving measures, such as low-flow toilets and faucets, and by selecting venues that use water-saving technologies and practices.

❖   Reducing energy consumption: Event planners can minimize energy consumption by using energy-efficient lighting and appliances, and by selecting venues with renewable energy sources, such as solar panels or wind turbines.

❖   Reducing carbon emissions: Event planners can reduce carbon emissions by selecting venues that are easily accessible by public transportation or that provide shuttle services, and by promoting carpooling amongst attendees.

❖   Promoting sustainable food options: Sustainable food options are those that are produced and distributed using environmentally-friendly practices, such as organic farming, fair labor practices, and local sourcing. By selecting sustainable food options for events, event planners can promote the environmental and social sustainability of their events.

Reducing Carbon Footprints

One of the main ways in which event planners can promote sustainability is by reducing the carbon footprint of their events.

Carbon footprint refers to the total amount of carbon dioxide and other greenhouse gases emitted by an event. Event planners can reduce the carbon footprint of their events by:

❖ Minimizing transportation emissions: Event planners can encourage attendees to carpool, use public transportation, or bike to events, in order to reduce transportation emissions. Additionally, they can offset the carbon emissions from attendee travel by purchasing carbon offsets.

❖ Using renewable energy sources: Event planners should select venues that use renewable energy sources, such as solar or wind power, or that have implemented energy-saving measures, such as LED lighting and energy-efficient appliances.

❖ Minimizing waste: Event planners should implement waste reduction practices, such as composting and recycling, and encourage attendees to do the same.

❖ Promoting environmental stewardship: Event planners can promote environmental stewardship by providing information and education on sustainability at events, and by engaging attendees in sustainable practices, such as volunteering at local environmental initiatives.

Working with Eco-Friendly Vendors

Another way in which event planners can promote sustainability is by working with eco-friendly vendors. Eco-friendly vendors are those that prioritize sustainable practices and are committed to minimizing their environmental impact. Event planners can select eco-friendly vendors for things like catering, decorations, and transportation. Additionally, they should ensure that vendors are aware of the event's sustainability goals and expectations.

Measuring the Impact of Sustainable Practices

Finally, event planners should measure the impact of their sustainable practices in order to assess their success and make adjustments as needed. This can be done through surveys and feedback forms, as well as by tracking metrics such as energy consumption and waste production. By measuring the impact of their sustainable practices, event planners can identify areas where they can improve and ensure that they are meeting their sustainability goals.

Conclusion

Sustainability in event planning is a critical component of responsible event planning. By embracing sustainable practices, event planners can reduce their events' environmental impact, promote social and economic sustainability, and create events that are both memorable and responsible. By integrating sustainability into their event planning process, event planners can ensure that their events have a positive impact on the world around them and contribute to a more sustainable future.

CHAPTER 13: RISK MANAGEMENT AND CONTINGENCY PLANNING

Events carry inherent risks, which must be identified, assessed, and adequately managed to ensure that the event runs smoothly. In this chapter, we will discuss the importance of risk management and contingency planning in event planning. We will outline the steps event planners should take, from risk identification to emergency response planning, to ensure a successful event.

Identifying Potential Risks and Hazards

Risk management begins with identifying potential risks and hazards associated with the event. Event planners should examine every aspect of the event, including the venue, the attendees, the weather, the vendors, the technology, and other relevant factors. This process should be thorough, and event planners should use checklists or templates to ensure they cover all the bases.

Some risks might include the following:

❖ Weather-related issues such as hurricanes, flooding, or

heatwaves

- ❖ Technical failures or IT malfunctions
- ❖ Fire or electrical hazards
- ❖ Food allergies or foodborne illnesses
- ❖ Security threats or potential violence
- ❖ Crowd-related issues, such as overcrowding or stampedes
- ❖ Health risks such as pandemics or contagious diseases.

Developing a Risk Management Plan

After identifying the potential risks, event planners should develop a risk management plan that outlines the steps for mitigating each risk. The risk management plan should be comprehensive and should cover pre-event, event, and post-event activities.

Pre-event Activities

Before the event, event planners should attempt to mitigate as many of the risks as possible. This might involve communicating with vendors, reviewing contracts, and conducting site visits to identify physical hazards such as faulty wiring or uneven terrain.

Event Activities

During the event, event planners should remain vigilant and implement the plan to mitigate any risks that may arise. Event planners should ensure that security measures are in place, and all attendees are aware of emergency procedures.

Post-event Activities

After the event, event planners should conduct an evaluation of the risk management plan. This evaluation will help ensure that the risk management plan remains relevant and up-to-date for future events.

Conducting Risk Assessments

Once the risk management plan is in place, event planners must conduct a risk assessment to identify areas of vulnerability. Risk assessments should be conducted at various stages of the event planning process.

Event planners should assess the following areas:

1. Physical Environment

Event planners must review the physical environment to identify any potential hazards or safety concerns. This includes reviewing the venue's safety policies, ensuring that fire alarms and sprinklers are working correctly, checking for tripping hazards, and reviewing access and egress points.

2. Vendors and Contractors

Event planners must assess the vendors and contractors to ensure that they have the necessary insurance, licenses, and permits. They should also review vendor contracts carefully to ensure that they comply with the risk management plan.

3. Personnel

Event planners should ensure that event staff has the necessary training and experience to manage the event safely. They should also assign specific roles and responsibilities to staff members to ensure that an appropriate response occurs in case of emergency.

4. Attendees

Event planners must assess attendees' needs, such as accessibility requirements and dietary restrictions, to ensure that they remain safe and protected at the event.

Creating Contingency Plans

Contingency plans are an essential aspect of event planning. A contingency plan outlines the steps that event planners should take in case of unexpected cancellation, postponement, or alteration of the event plan. Event planners should establish contingency plans at various stages of the event planning process.

1. Pre-Event Contingency Plans

Pre-event contingency plans should detail the steps event planners will take if risks are identified before the event. This might include identifying alternate event locations, reviewing vendor contracts, and developing backup plans if the primary supplier is unavailable.

2. Event Contingency Plans

Event contingency plans should outline the steps that event planners will take in case of an emergency during the event. This includes developing evacuation plans, identifying medical facilities' locations, and establishing a process for communicating emergency protocols to event attendees.

3. Post-event Contingency Plans

Post-event contingency plans should detail the steps for managing the aftermath of the event. This might include tracking incidents, conducting a crisis debriefing, and handling liability claims.

Developing Emergency Response Plans

Emergency response plans are critical components of risk management and contingency planning. An emergency response plan outlines the steps to take in case of an unexpected emergency such as natural disasters, security breaches, or other major incidents. It should include the following:

1. Establishing Emergency Teams

Event planners should create an emergency response team that includes the following:

- ❖ Incident commander
- ❖ Security team
- ❖ Medical staff
- ❖ Evacuation team
- ❖ Logistics and coordination team.

2. Developing Response Protocols

The emergency response plan should include protocols for responding to different types of emergencies. Protocols should include communication plans, medical treatment procedures, evacuation procedures, and crowd management procedures.

3. Communicating Emergency Protocols

The emergency response plan should be communicated effectively to all parties involved, including staff, vendors, and attendees. This might include distributing emergency response cards or placing emergency response signage throughout the venue.

4. Testing the Plan

Event planners should conduct regular simulations of the emergency response plan to identify weaknesses and gaps in the plan. This might include mock evacuations, simulations of emergency medical situations, or other emergency scenarios.

Conclusion

Risk management and contingency planning are vital components of event planning. The ability to respond quickly and effectively in case of an emergency is essential to ensure the safety of event attendees and staff. By identifying potential risks and developing comprehensive risk management and contingency plans, event planners can minimize the negative impact of unpredicted events and ensure a successful event.

CHAPTER 14: TEAM MANAGEMENT AND LEADERSHIP

Event planning is a team sport, and success depends on the people working together towards a common goal. A great team is the lifeblood of successful event planning, and team management and leadership are crucial to creating a cohesive and effective workforce.

In this chapter, we will discuss the key leadership skills necessary for event planning and highlight ways to develop and maintain a high-performing team. We will explore approaches to motivate team members and ways to deal with conflict. We will examine ways to provide feedback and recognition, and ways to develop leadership skills among team members. Finally, we will discuss ways to maintain cohesion during high-stress situations and how to build a strong team network.

Identifying Key Leadership Skills

The ability to lead, mentor, and inspire a team is essential to successful event planning. While many of the skills used by successful leaders are transferable from other industries, there are some specific skill sets that are required to excel in event planning.

Visionary thinking, strategic planning, and problem-solving are at the top of the list. A great event planner should be able to visualize the big picture and work to create a road map of how to achieve the event's end goal. They must be able to think critically about potential roadblocks and develop creative solutions to move forward.

Excellent communication and collaboration skills are also critical. Great leaders in event planning must be able to communicate and collaborate with people from all walks of life, from clients to vendors to guests to their team. They must be able to build relationships with these stakeholders to achieve the event's objectives.

Another essential trait of great event planners is flexibility and adaptability. No two events are quite the same, and things rarely go exactly as planned. A great event planner must be able to adjust course quickly and efficiently, drawing on creativity, problem-solving skills, and adaptability.

Creating a Strong Team Culture

A successful event is the result of an exceptional team. The best event planners understand that it's not just about the individual talents of each employee, but it's about creating a team culture that fosters innovation, collaboration, and teamwork.

To create a strong team culture, leaders must clearly define the team's purpose and mission and encourage the team to buy into that mission. Leaders must also promote an environment of open communication, where everyone feels comfortable sharing their thoughts and ideas. Team members should feel comfortable stepping outside their comfort zones, taking risks, and innovating.

Effective team leaders also take the time to learn about their staff not only as employees but as people. They must pay attention to the interests, ambitions, and challenges of each employee, and develop a personal relationship with them.

Motivating Team Members

To create a driven and dedicated team, effective team leaders are motivating and inspiring. Positive reinforcement, clear communication, and leading by example are some of the ways you can motivate your team.

One of the most effective ways to motivates teams is to set clear and realistic goals. These goals should be challenging enough to require effort, but not so difficult that they discourage team members. When you meet these goals, you should recognize and reward team members for their accomplishments, such as public recognition, bonuses, or additional responsibilities.

Another way to inspire your team is by leading by example. If you are asking your team to work long hours or put in extra effort, it's essential that you demonstrate the same work ethic and energy. By working alongside your team members, they will see your dedication and be motivated to match it.

Managing Conflict Within Teams

Conflict is a reality in any workplace, and event planning is no exception. In fact, event planning can be especially stressful leading to conflict. As a team leader, it's essential to develop a strategy for dealing with conflict.

The first step in dealing with conflict is to address it immediately. Don't allow it to fester and grow into greater problems. Encourage open communication and active listening so that both parties can express their viewpoints calmly and respectfully.

Another way to approach conflict resolution is by implementing a formal conflict resolution plan. This plan should detail the steps and procedures for dealing with different forms of conflict and should be made available to all team members.

Providing Feedback and Recognition

Providing feedback and recognition are essential when managing a team. Individuals need to know how they are performing, identify areas for improvement, and get the recognition they deserve when it's warranted.

Constructive feedback should be specific and timely and delivered with a solution-focused approach. Avoid criticism that could put an employee on the back foot or make them defensive about their performance. Instead, focus on specific examples of where someone is excelling and where improvement is necessary.

Recognition can be a powerful motivator for team members-the simple act of acknowledging accomplishments can boost morale, improve productivity, and increase the team's alignment around common goals. Recognition can come in different forms, from a public acknowledgment during a team meeting to company-wide recognition programs.

Developing Leadership Skills Among Team Members.

Effective event planners understand the value of developing leadership skills among their teams. By investing in leadership training and supporting the development of rising stars, companies build capacity and position themselves for long-term success.

To develop your team members' leadership skills, you should provide leadership training opportunities, opportunities to take ownership or lead projects, coaching, and access to mentors. You can also give team members rotating leadership roles so that they can gain experience managing different aspects of an event.

Maintaining Cohesion During High-Stress Situations

In the world of event planning, stress is an inevitable part of the job. From last-minute vendor cancellations to guest complaints, stress can occur at any time. However, great leaders know how to react positively to high-stress situations and keep their team cohesive.

To deal with high-stress situations, event leaders should lead by example, remain calm under pressure, and communicate transparently with their teams, vendors, and clients. Additionally, team members should not be overworked or put under undue pressure, leading to burnout. Instead, provide an environment to take a break from work, such as a relaxing space or schedule changes with advance notice.

Building a Strong Team Network

Effective event planning is not possible with a weak team network. To build a strong team network, you should focus on building relationships, which can be achieved through networking events, industry conferences, and company events.

Building strong relationships within your network is about creating a strong foundation of trust that fosters long-term partnerships. Whether it's collaborating with vendors or cultivating relationships with representatives from local industry associations, networking opportunities, and events can help grow your network.

Conclusion

Effective team management and leadership are critical to successful event planning. Leaders must cultivate a strong team culture, motivate team members, deal with conflict, and provide feedback and recognition. Developing leadership skills among team members is crucial, as is maintaining cohesion during stressful periods and building a strong team network.

When teams are motivated, innovative, and working together

towards common goals, the possibilities to create unforgettable events are endless. Invest in your team and give them the resources, support, and recognition they need to achieve great things.

CHAPTER 15: EVENT TRENDS AND INNOVATIONS

Successful event planners need to stay up-to-date on the latest trends and innovations in the industry. Incorporating new ideas and techniques can make events stand out and provide unique experiences for attendees. In this chapter, we will explore some of the most popular trends and innovations in event planning.

Identifying current event trends

In order to stay relevant, event planners must keep an eye on current trends in the industry. One of the biggest trends in recent years has been the rise of experiential events. Attendees don't just want to attend an event – they want to be fully immersed in it. This means creating interactive experiences, like virtual reality or augmented reality, that allow guests to engage with the event on a deeper level.

Another trend that has been gaining popularity is the use of pop-up events. These temporary experiences can be used to build buzz or anticipation for a future event, or to add an element of surprise to an otherwise ordinary location. Pop-up events can range from art installations to food trucks, and can be tailored to fit any event theme.

Incorporating cutting-edge technology

Technology is constantly advancing, and event planners need to keep up with the latest trends and innovations in order to provide the best experience for attendees. One popular use of technology in event planning is the use of mobile apps. Event apps can be customized to fit each event's unique needs, providing attendees with schedules, maps, and interactive features that enhance the event experience.

In addition to mobile apps, event planners are also incorporating new types of technology like facial recognition and biometric scanning. These technologies can help with event security and access control, and can streamline the check-in process for attendees.

Developing immersive experiences

For events to be truly memorable, they need to provide guests with immersive experiences that engage all five senses. This means incorporating elements like sound, lighting, and scent into the event design. For example, a fashion show may use specific lighting to highlight certain aspects of the clothes being showcased, while a food festival may use rich scents to entice attendees to try different dishes.

Creating pop-up events

Pop-up events have become incredibly popular in recent years, and for good reason. These temporary experiences can be used to build excitement for an upcoming event, or to provide a one-of-a-kind experience for attendees. From food trucks to art installations, pop-up events can be customized to fit any event theme or type.

Utilizing event themes

An event theme can tie everything together and provide a cohesive experience for attendees. Themes can range from simple color schemes to more complex ideas, like a "under the sea" event that incorporates oceanic elements throughout the design. Event planners should choose a theme that fits the event and audience and use it to guide everything from décor to marketing materials.

Implementing food and beverage trends

Food and beverage options can play a big role in event success, and event planners need to stay on top of current trends to provide the best options for attendees. One trend that has been gaining popularity is the use of local ingredients and locally sourced foods. Attendees are becoming more conscious of where their food comes from, and incorporating local elements into the menu can make the event feel more authentic and unique.

Creating sensory experiences

Sensory experiences are a powerful way to engage attendees and create an immersive event environment. These experiences can incorporate elements like sound, lighting, and scent to create a multi-dimensional experience that engages all five senses. Event planners should work with vendors and design teams to create sensory experiences that fit the event theme and provide a unique experience for attendees.

Fostering community engagement

Events are a great way to bring people together, and event planners should look for ways to foster community engagement at their events. This can involve creating interactive experiences or activities that encourage people to interact with each other, like games or challenges. Event planners should also look for ways to incorporate social media into the event, using hashtags and other tools to encourage attendees to post and share their experiences online.

Conclusion

Staying on top of current trends and innovations in event planning is essential for success in the industry. From creating immersive experiences to incorporating cutting-edge technology, event planners should always be looking for new ideas and techniques that can enhance the event experience for attendees. By staying up-to-date on current trends, event planners can stay ahead of the competition and provide truly memorable events that keep attendees coming back year after year.

CHAPTER 16: LEGAL AND ETHICAL CONSIDERATIONS

As an event planner, it is important to understand and adhere to legal and ethical considerations to ensure the success of the event and avoid any legal or ethical issues. In this chapter, we will discuss the various legal and ethical considerations that need to be taken into account while planning an event.

Understanding Legal Requirements for Event Planning

Every event is governed by different laws and regulations, and it is essential for event planners to understand them to avoid any legal issues. The legal requirements for events may vary depending on the city, state, or country in which the event is taking place. For example, in some areas, outdoor events require specific permits, or if alcohol is being served at the event, then a liquor license may be needed. Event planners must research and follow all of the applicable laws and regulations to ensure that they remain in compliance.

Reviewing Contracts and Agreements

Contracts and agreements are an essential aspect of event planning. An event planner must create contracts for vendors, sponsors, and participants that define all the details of their agreements. These contracts can include payment details, services provided, duration of the agreement, cancellation policies, and legal disclaimers.

An event planner must also review contracts with the venue to ensure that the terms and conditions of the agreement are fair, that the venue meets the needs of the event, and that the contract covers any issues that may arise. Contracts are vital for protecting all parties involved in the event.

Ensuring Compliance with Regulations

Event planners must ensure compliance with the regulations to avoid any legal risks. The regulations vary from event to event, depending on the location, type of event, and number of attendees. For example, an indoor event may need to comply with fire safety regulations, accessibility requirements, and noise ordinances. An outdoor event may have to adhere to more regulations such as crowd control and traffic management. Event planners must review and follow all the regulations to ensure the safety and success of the event.

Handling Intellectual Property Issues

An event planner must protect intellectual property in order to avoid any legal issues. Intellectual property can include copyrighted music, images, or video content that may be used during the event. It's important for the event planner to obtain permissions from the owners or creators of the content being used during the event.

Maintaining Ethical Standards

Event planners must comply with ethical considerations while planning an event. It's important to consider the ethics of the event, including cultural and social sensitivities, and how the event may affect the community or environment.

Protecting Event Attendees' Personal Information

Event attendees' personal information, such as addresses, email addresses, and phone numbers, must be kept confidential. An event planner must take appropriate measures to protect the data, such as limiting access to personal information and storing it securely.

Managing Liability Risks

Event planners must take appropriate measures to manage liability risks. They must have liability insurance to cover damages received as a result of the event. In addition, they should identify potential risks and hazards during the event planning process and take appropriate measures to mitigate those risks.

Dealing with Insurance Concerns

Event planners must make sure they have the appropriate insurance coverage for the event. The type of coverage needed is based on the type of event, its location, and the number of attendees. Insurance coverage can include liability coverage, cancellation coverage, property damage coverage, and workers' compensation coverage.

Conclusion

Legal and ethical considerations are critical to planning a successful event. By following the laws, regulations, contracts, and agreements that govern events, event planners can minimize legal risks and ensure that their events meet the high standards of ethical conduct. Understanding the legal and ethical considerations of event planning is essential for protecting both the event planner and the attendees and ensuring the success of

RAY GOODWIN

the event.

CHAPTER 17: INTERNATIONAL EVENT PLANNING

As the world becomes more interconnected, event planners are increasingly tasked with organizing events that span borders and cultures. International event planning poses unique challenges, from navigating language barriers to understanding local customs and regulations. In this chapter, we'll explore the key skills and strategies required for successful international event planning.

Understanding cultural differences

When planning an event in a foreign country, it's important to be aware of and respect cultural differences. What may be considered acceptable or even expected behavior in one country can be viewed as rude or offensive in another. Take the time to research the customs and traditions of the country you'll be visiting, as well as the cultural backgrounds of your attendees and stakeholders. This will help you avoid any unintentional cultural faux-pas.

Preparing for international travel

Travel logistics can be especially challenging when organizing an international event. In addition to booking flights and hotels, you'll need to consider visa requirements, vaccinations, and any travel advisories or restrictions. It's also a good idea to research local transportation options and learn how to navigate public transit systems.

Conducting site visits abroad

Site visits are an essential part of event planning, allowing you to get a sense of the event space and facilities. When planning an international event, it's important to conduct site visits in person to get an accurate sense of the space and its capabilities, as well as to meet with local vendors and partners. This may require additional travel and logistics planning, but it's a necessary step to ensure the success of your event.

Adapting event formats to different cultures

The format and structure of events can vary widely from country to country. For example, a formal sit-down dinner may be expected in one country, while a casual buffet might be more appropriate in another. Be prepared to adapt your event format to align with cultural norms and expectations. It can be helpful to seek the advice of local partners or colleagues to ensure your event is respectful and appropriate.

Working with international vendors and partners

When planning an international event, you'll likely need to work with local vendors and partners. This can include catering services, AV and technical support, and transportation providers. It's important to research and vet potential vendors to ensure they have experience working with international clients and can meet your specific needs. Language barriers can also be a challenge when working with international partners, so consider hiring a translator or interpreter if necessary.

Managing language and communication barriers

Effective communication is a key component of any successful event planning endeavor. When working across languages and cultures, it's important to be aware of language barriers and take steps to ensure clear communication. This can include hiring translators or using language translation software, as well as being mindful of differences in communication styles.

Securing necessary visas and permits

Depending on the location of your event, you may need to obtain visas or permits to enter the country, as well as any necessary permits for event activities. Understanding local regulations and requirements is essential to ensuring your event can go smoothly. This can include working with local partners or hiring legal experts to navigate any legal and regulatory requirements.

Planning for international emergencies

No matter how well you plan, unforeseen emergencies can and do happen. When planning an international event, it's important to have a comprehensive emergency plan in place to address any potential issues. This can include communication plans, contingency plans for unexpected changes to the event, and plans for handling medical emergencies or natural disasters.

International event planning can be a complex and challenging endeavor, but with the right skills and strategies, it can also be incredibly rewarding. By preparing ahead of time, adapting to local customs and regulations, and working with experienced partners and vendors, you can ensure your event is a success no matter where in the world it takes place.

CHAPTER 18: NON-PROFIT EVENT PLANNING

When it comes to event planning for non-profit organizations, the goal is to create an event that not only meets the client's objectives but also raises funds for their cause. As an event planner, it is important to understand the client's mission and values so that the event can align with their overall goals. Here are some key points to consider when planning a non-profit event:

- ❖ Identifying non-profit goals: At the outset, it is crucial to understand the client's goals. What do they hope to achieve with the event? Is the aim to raise awareness, raise funds, or to engage with donors and supporters? The answers to these questions will influence the planning process and help to identify the types of activities, fundraising techniques, and communication strategies that can be used.

- ❖ Creating a fundraising strategy: One of the primary goals of most non-profit events is to raise funds. As an event planner, you need to work closely with the client to develop a fundraising strategy that is aligned with their goals. This can involve using different techniques like online fundraising, silent auctions, and raffles to encourage guests to donate. The fundraiser should be highlighted prominently in the event agenda, and attendees should be encouraged to give generously.

❖   Working with donors and sponsors: Depending on the non-profit's size and reach, it may be necessary to secure sponsors and donors for the event. As an event planner, it is your responsibility to identify potential sponsors and donors, develop a sponsorship strategy, and create compelling proposals. You can also promote the non-profit's values and mission while maintaining transparency in all dealings.

❖   Promoting non-profit missions: In non-profit events, it is important to remind attendees why they are there. Raising awareness for the non-profit's mission is critical, and this can be achieved through engaging speakers, live performances, or video presentations. These elements can help to convey the non-profit's message in a compelling and memorable way.

❖   Managing volunteer relationships: Volunteers are often the backbone of non-profit events, and their roles are crucial to delivering a successful event. As an event planner, it is important to ensure that volunteers feel valued and appreciated. You can achieve this by offering them the necessary resources, training, and support they need to succeed. Communicating clearly and effectively is also key, as it helps to avoid any misunderstandings or confusion among volunteers.

❖   Coordinating events with non-profit missions: Non-profit events should be integrated with the mission of the organization. The themes, activities, and speakers should align with the organization's goals. This serves to reiterate the non-profit's values and goals while honoring attendees and donors.

❖   Establishing partnerships with other non-profits: Collaboration is critical in the non-profit sector. Event planners can work towards establishing partnerships with other non-profits, which will create opportunities to combine skills, resources, and contacts that can be leveraged to support the mission of non-profits.

❖ Conducting post-event evaluations: For event planners, the success of a non-profit event is directly tied to how well it meets the client's objectives. Using post-event evaluations, it is possible to gauge the impact of the event. This information can provide valuable insights into the effectiveness of the event, suggest areas for improvement, and lay down a solid foundation for future events.

Conclusion

Non-profit event planning can be daunting, but with thorough planning and careful attention to the client's objectives, a successful event can be created. Understanding the client's mission, identifying fundraising goals and strategies, working with donors and sponsors, promoting non-profit missions, coordinating with volunteers, creating engaging activities, and developing strong partnerships with other non-profits are some of the steps that can be taken to create an unforgettable event. Finally, it is important to conduct a post-event evaluation to understand the impact of the event and to constantly refine your approach.

CHAPTER 19: EVENT PLANNING FOR CORPORATE CLIENTS

In this chapter, we will focus on event planning for corporate clients. Corporate events can vary widely from team-building events to major product launches and annual meetings. As an event planner, you need to have a clear understanding of your corporate client's goals, objectives, and expectations. Additionally, you should be prepared to provide a wide range of services to satisfy the needs of your corporate clients.

Understanding Corporate Event Planning Goals:

Corporate events have specific goals that must be met to achieve success. As an event planner, you have to understand these goals to plan a successful event. The goals for corporate events differ depending on the type of event and the client. Some corporate events are intended to build relationships between company employees, while others are designed to launch a new product, entertain clients, or showcase new innovations or technology. It's important to understand corporate goals in order to meet the objectives of their event.

Working with Corporate Clients:

Corporate clients often require a higher level of service,

professionalism, and attention to detail, compared to other clients. As an event planner, you must be able to work directly with corporate clients and be familiar with the corporate culture. Communication with corporate clients is essential to ensure that their needs and goals are met. It's important to listen to their requests and suggestions and provide innovative ideas and timely feedback.

Creating Team Building Events:

Team building events are becoming increasingly popular in the corporate world. Team building is designed to bring employees together and promote teamwork and communication. As an event planner, you should offer innovative ideas and team building games and activities that cater to your clients' needs. Event planners can organize workshops that address new ways to manage problems, improve communication skills, and promote team-building.

Organizing Product Launches:

Product launches are an important part of the corporate world. When a company is launching a new product, there's a need to get consumer attention. As an event planner, you must create a unique product launch event to catch people's attention. Successful product launches often have a specific theme, visual presentation, and interactive events that are unforgettable.

Organizing Annual Meetings:

Annual meetings are an excellent way for corporate clients to communicate with employees and shareholders. These events bring people together to discuss financial and business strategies. Event planners should be involved in the planning process to ensure that the event runs smoothly. It's important to consider event venues that provide great amenities so that the attendees have everything they need to participate in the meeting.

Conducting Incentive Trips:

Incentive trips are designed to motivate employees for better performance. These events are often organized as a reward for the best-performing staff members. Incentive trips can be either local or international, which gives employees an opportunity to experience new cultures and see different parts of the world. As an event planner, it's essential to create a unique and immersive experience that will motivate employees.

Providing Entertainment and Keynote Speakers:

Entertainment and keynote speakers are vital elements in corporate events. As an event planner, you should suggest unique entertainment options that will create a memorable experience for guests. Additionally, keynote speakers should be engaging, inspirational, and knowledgeable to maintain the attention of the attendees throughout the event.

Measuring Corporate Event Success:

Measuring corporate event success involves gathering feedback from attendees, corporate clients, and sponsors. This feedback should include clear, measurable goals that were achieved and suggestions for improvement. As an event planner, you should develop and present an event report that outlines event goals, attendees' feedback, and areas for improvement.

In conclusion, Corporate events are an excellent way for companies to communicate their goals and objectives to employees, shareholders, and business partners. As an event planner, it's your duty to ensure that the event is successful, meets client goals, and achieves its objectives. Working with corporate clients requires patience, creativity, and a high level of professionalism. You should listen to your clients' needs and provide innovative ideas and solutions that meet their expectations. Finally, measuring the success of the event will help you improve your planning process and create better events in the future.

CHAPTER 20: CAREER DEVELOPMENT IN EVENT PLANNING

Event planning is an exciting and creative field that requires hard work, dedication, and passion. As an event planner, you are responsible for bringing people together and creating memorable experiences. In this chapter, we will explore the different career paths in event planning, how to gain valuable experience, and tips for success.

Identifying Career Paths in Event Planning

Event planning offers a wide range of career paths, from entry-level positions to management roles. Entry-level positions include event coordinator and event assistant, while management roles include event manager, senior event manager, and event director. Other positions include marketing coordinator, social media manager, sponsorship manager, and production manager. In each of these roles, there are opportunities for specialization, such as weddings, corporate events, and non-profit events.

Gaining Event Planning Experience

Experience is key in the event planning industry. To gain experience, consider volunteering at local events or interning with event planning companies. This will give you hands-on experience and the opportunity to network with industry professionals. Additionally, consider taking on event planning projects for family and friends, as this can help you develop your skills and build your portfolio.

Building a Professional Network

Networking is important in any industry, and event planning is no exception. Attend industry events, join professional organizations such as the Event Planning Association (EPA), and connect with other event planners on social media platforms. Building a strong professional network can lead to new opportunities and valuable resources.

Attaining Certification and Continuing Education

Becoming certified as an event planner can help demonstrate your qualifications and expertise in the field. The Certified Meeting Professional (CMP) credential, offered by the Events Industry Council, is a widely recognized certification in the event planning industry. Continuing education is also important in event planning, as it can help you stay up-to-date on industry trends and best practices. Consider attending conferences, workshops, and webinars to expand your knowledge and skills.

Developing Leadership and Management Skills

Leadership and management skills are essential for success in event planning. As you gain experience, look for opportunities to manage a team or take on a leadership role. Additionally, consider taking courses in management and leadership to develop your skills. Effective communication, problem-solving, and time management skills are also crucial for success in this field.

Creating a Personal Brand

Creating a personal brand can help you stand out in the event planning industry. Your personal brand should reflect your values, skills, and experience. This can include creating a professional website, developing a strong social media presence, and showcasing your work through a portfolio. Your personal brand should also include a clear message about who you are and what you can offer as an event planner.

Pursuing Entrepreneurial Opportunities in Event Planning

Starting your own event planning business can be a rewarding and challenging opportunity. This can allow you to work on your own schedule, develop your own client base, and focus on the types of events that interest you the most. However, starting a business requires careful planning, financial management, and marketing skills. Consider taking courses or working with a mentor to develop your entrepreneurial skills.

Tips for Success as an Event Planner

➢ Develop strong relationships with clients and vendors

➢ Communicate effectively with your team and clients

➢ Stay organized and detail-oriented

➢ Be adaptable and flexible in the face of unexpected changes

➢ Keep up-to-date on industry trends and best practices

➢ Build a strong professional network

➢ Develop your leadership and management skills

➢ Be passionate and enthusiastic about your work

Conclusion

Event planning is a dynamic and exciting field that offers a variety of career paths and opportunities for growth. To be successful, it is important to gain valuable experience, build a strong professional network, and continue your education and development. With hard work, dedication, and a passion for creating memorable experiences, you can build a successful career in event planning.

Final Thoughts

As we come to the end of this book, I hope that you have gained valuable insights on how to plan successful events. Event planning is a complex and challenging task, but with the right mindset, skills, and strategies, it can be a fulfilling and rewarding experience.

In today's fast-paced world where people have busy schedules, events are an important way of bringing people together to socialize, network, celebrate or learn. As an event planner, your role is critical in ensuring that these occasions run smoothly and achieve their objectives.

Remember that every event is unique; therefore, it requires personalized attention and creativity. The key to success lies in understanding the needs of your clients, being flexible and adaptable to changes and challenges that may arise during the planning process.

Also essential is fostering healthy relationships with vendors and team members as they play a significant part in making your event successful.

I encourage you not only to use this book as a guide but also to embrace every opportunity for learning and growth in your journey as an event planner. With passion, vision, hard work and dedication towards creating unforgettable experiences for your clients—the possibilities are endless.

ABOUT THE AUTHOR

Ray Goodwin

Ray Goodwin, is the author behind this series of captivating books on Business Development and self improvement, and has left an indelible mark on the field. He was born and raised in the bustling city of London, where he developed a strong work ethic and an insatiable curiosity about the inner workings of successful businesses. Throughout his illustrious career, Ray leveraged his extensive knowledge and experience to help numerous companies flourish and prosper.

His keen insights and innovative strategies has earned him recognition, driving him to share his expertise with others. Ray believes in the power of sharing knowledge to elevate businesses and empower aspiring entrepreneurs.

Ray's dedication to his craft is evident in the numerous books he has authored on business development and self improvement. His writing style seamlessly blends practical advice, thought-provoking concepts, and real-life case studies, making his books invaluable resources for business professionals and novices alike. His ability to distill complex concepts into accessible language has greatly impacted the lives and careers of countless individuals.

Now retired from the corporate world, Ray and his beloved wife have settled in the idyllic English countryside. Surrounded by the beauty of nature, Ray finds inspiration for his writing and indulges in his hobbies.

Ray Goodwin's books continue to serve as enduring guides for those seeking success in the business world. With a wealth of experience and a deep understanding of the inner workings of businesses, Ray's work remains a testament to his passion for sharing knowledge and helping others flourish.